Pag
Part I: Þrymskviða

By Varg Vikernes & Marie Cachet

Initial Notes

My contribution to this (the first one in a series) have mainly been to translate the Norse stanzas, to find the etymological meanings to some of the different names and to write the English text. The *Maïeutics* itself is mainly the work of my wife, Marie.

Varg Vikernes
July 2017

Shadows Dancing on the Wall

Imagine that you are a child again and you still believe in "Santa Claus". When your parents tell you about the Yule traditions, you see them from the perspective of a child. Innocent, but also ignorant. When you grow older you *understand* that there is no "Santa Claus", and you see reality. You have passed a test. You have turned around and can now see what is causing the shadows on the wall in front of you to dance.

Our mythology must be understood in this light. The purpose is not to make people believe in fictional entities and fantastical events. The purpose is not to make people believe the shadows dancing on the wall are real. The purpose is to educate and to distinguish the wheat from the tares.

This explains the purpose of our mythology, but it also explains *why* the Tradition of our forebears was replaced by Christianity and some places Islam. The

Native European Tradition was a system of tests, and only the best would pass those tests and become initiated. When the Native European man diminished, because of the domestication of animals, agriculture and later civilization, fewer and fewer Native Europeans were able to pass those tests, and to more and more of them their Tradition remained "a belief in Santa Claus".

Before we continue, let me explain briefly why and how the domestication of animals, agriculture and later civilization diminished the Native European man. In short, this brought an easier life and a much more comfortable life. The natural selection that the nomadic hunter-gatherer lifestyle had ensured was removed. Life became *too* easy and *too* comfortable, and the Native European man began to domesticate himself. This auto-domestication in turn lead to a dramatical lowering of the intelligence level of the Native European man.

Because of that auto-domestication, gradually, over time, more and more Native Europeans *failed* to turn around and see that caused the shadows to dance on the wall in front of them. Even in the Classical Antiquity, the Native European Tradition had lost almost all meaning to the vast majority of Native Europeans. It offered close to nothing to them. The majority had become too simple minded to discover it's deeper meaning.

Thus when Christianity arrived, it was *possible* to replace the Native European Tradition. The average man still believed in "Santa Claus", so to speak, and thus could be duped, bribed, threatened or forced to accept a new faith, with promises that were much more attractive than that silly belief in "Santa Claus".

The new faith from the desert had little real content too, it had the depth of a shallow bath dub, so the Native European man *kept* his Native European Traditions, even though he officially had accepted a new faith. Therefore we see today a Christianity so steeped in Pagan Traditions, celebrating Pagan high festivals and Pagan Gods and Goddesses as "Saints" (like the well known "Santa Claus"), and incorporating Pagan myths, song, stories and even ideals. Because of that, we are even today able to explain the Native European Tradition, from A to Z.

Maïeutics

Maïeutics, a term for "midwifery", is (here) a name for a Socratic method of "giving birth to minds". Maïa, a Native European goddess, is the midwife helping the mother give birth, and we intend with these books "to help give birth to minds", by unveiling *the secrets* of our forebears.

Before any Maïeutics can begin though, we need to "cut through the crap" that has been firmly placed in between us and our own heritage, by the Christians and scholars. Ever since the beginning of the

Christianization of Europe the intentional falsification and Christianization of our heritage has poisoned the well of knowledge. This poisoning continued during and after the Renaissance (a revival of our own heritage) and even into modern times. Whatever was written by our forebears, was interpreted in a Christian light. Whatever was found from the pre-Christian era, was analysed from a Christian perspective. E. g. even though our forebears, from all over Europe, tell us *plain and clear* that they believed in *reincarnation*, the Christians interpreted the myths and traditions and graves and tales as if our forebears believed in a " heavenly afterlife". Also, the European deities were looked upon like the Christians view their own Hebrew God.

But our forebears did *not* believe that the dead brought with them all the things they were buried with to some "heavenly afterlife". Their deities were *not* anything like the Hebrew God. Their myths were *not* "creation myths". Loki was *not* "their devil". And so forth.

Yet, even today the scholars ignore the obvious and well documented fact that *our forebears believed in reincarnation*. As we will show you, the evidence is all over our mythology, our myths, in historical records, in archaeology, in songs and in traditions. But the scholars refuse to see, because they are *locked* in their *Christian* perspective.

When they interpret everything from the obviously wrong perspective, then of course everything they say and write about this becomes nothing short of misinformation. They educate themselves and others to ignorance. They learn and parrot lies. They cover our entire heritage in mud.

So before we begin, please let us help you wash away the mud, and start with clean sheets. "Unlearn" what the scholars have taught you, and be ready to see our heritage for what it is.

Hamingja

As we will show you with this book series, to our Pagan forebears the physical death was only the death of the physical shape, and your spirit would keep on existing. Therefore they talked about e. g. *Hamhleypa* ("running in shapes") and *Hamingja* ("walk in shapes"). You, the real *you*, was a spirit, and life was just "a walk in physical shapes". Every time your body died, you would leave it, before you were reborn again, in a new body.

In order for the spirit to return to life, in order for you to be reincarnated ("be given a new physical body"), you had to find back to yourself. This was important, because your memories were stored not in any part of your physical body, but in your spirit. So finding back to yourself was not just about "returning to life", but mainly about remembering past lives – past experiences. It was about you remembering what you knew before. Now, how useful would not that have been, if you could *remember* what you knew and learned in previous lives? Instead of having to start every life on bare ground, you could build on, from where you had left in the previous life.

As we will show you with this book series, our myths, our fairy tales, and our whole tradition therefore revolves around this concept: of you finding back to yourself.

The Science of Patterns

As you will see, our forebears knew a lot more than people today give them credit for. They even knew things that we today are only able to know because of *modern* science. Many will not accept what we say in our books because of that. "How could they know?" Well, they knew because they understood that they were a part of nature (and not above it, like Christians think), and they studied the *patterns* of nature. Thus they could e. g. understand that liquid runs through the branches of a tree, because the tree looks like the blood vessels of our bodies, and like rivers in the valley below. Same pattern, same function. Same function, same pattern. They could further e. g. understand that the bear mates in the spring and summer, but does not have a developed fetus until after it starts to hibernate (around Halloween). And regardless of the moment of mating, they all give birth to their cubs at the same time (around Yule). They could see that the fat she-bears had many cubs, and the others few or even none. So they could understand that the she-bear could "freeze" the embryos and later decide how many she would develop based on how much fat she had on her body. You don't need a microscope to understand that, you can simply just observe nature and use your head. And that is what they did. That is *how* they were able to understand so much.

Gods & Goddesses

Our forebears' belief in spirits and reincarnation naturally comes into conflict with what Christians/scholars tell us about their deities. Not because there is a real discrepancy there, but because what they tell us is simply not correct. The Christians/scholars know only the belief in "Santa Claus", and then do their best to misrepresent that, and we end up with an image of Pagans thinking the gods rode wagons in the sky and ripped one eye out and threw it into a well, or with talking severed heads and beautiful goddesses sleeping with dwarves or eight-legged horses born by a god and magic hammers, and men turned into stone by the gaze of the Medusa and so forth. They even go look for a real historical city called Troy, because they have not understood *anything*. Their entire effort is based around locating where "Santa Claus" lives, so to speak.

So, *starting* with this little booklet, we will systematically unveil the deities of our ancestors, show their nature, show their purposes, show their meaning and show you the true European Tradition. We begin with Þrymskviða, but will try to cover as much as we can, as much as we can find the time for in this life.

Because our Native European heritage is pan-European, with only flavour differences from North to South, and from East to West, we will talk about fairy tales, myths, traditions, songs and archaeological finds from all over Europe – and sometimes even from beyond, to areas where Native Europeans used to live in the past.

On the following pages, you will find Þrymskviða in both Norse (the language it was recorded in) and English. In the end you will find an interpretation by my wife.

Þrymskviða

1.

Vreiðr var þá Vingþórr
er hann vaknaði
ok síns hamars
of saknaði,
skegg nam at hrista,
skör nam at dýja,
réð Jarðar burr
um at þreifask.

1. Ox-Þórr was angry
when he woke up,
and missed
his hammer/rock.
He shook his beard,
he shook his head/hair,
the son of Earth
started to feel around (with his hands).

The name Ving-Þórr is often translated as "Ving-Þórr",
but the Ving- prefix means "ox", so I use the term "Ox-
Þórr" here. The name Þórr itself means "thunder".

2.

Ok hann þat orða
alls fyrst of kvað:
"Heyrðu nú, Loki,
hvat ek nú mæli
er eigi veit
jarðar hvergi
né upphimins:
áss er stolinn hamri!"

2.

And he the words
first of all said:
"Hear Loki,
hear what I say,
that nobody on Earth
or in the high heavens know:
they have stolen the stone/hammer
from the spirit".

Norse *áss* derives from proto-Nordic *ansuR*, from proto-Germanic *ansuz*, meaning "spirit", but it is generally understood by scholars as being the name for the Norse gods.

3.

Gengu þeir fagra
Freyju túna,
ok hann þat orða
alls fyrst of kvað:
"Muntu mér, Freyja,
fjaðrhams léa,
ef ek minn hamar
mættak hitta?".

3.

They went to fair
Freyja in the courtyard,
and he the words
first of all said:
"Will you, Freyja,
let me borrow your
feather-shape
so that I can find my hammer?"

Freyja kvað:

4.
"Þó munda ek gefa þér
þótt ór gulli væri,
ok þó selja,
at væri ór silfri."

Freyja said:

4.
"I gave it to you with pleasure,
even if it had been made of gold,
and let you have it
even if it had been made of silver."

5.
Fló þá Loki,
- fjaðrhamr dunði, -
unz fyr útan kom
ása garða
ok fyr innan kom
jötna heima.

5.

Loki then flew
- the feather-shape thundered -
until he left
the yard of the spirits
and he came into
the home of the ettins.

6.

Þrymr sat á haugi,
þursa dróttinn,
greyjum sínum
gullbönd sneri
ok mörum sínum
mön jafnaði.

6.

Þrymr ("Rumble") sat on the mound
the king of noise,
he made golden cords
for his dogs
and combed the manes of
his horses.

Þrymr kvað:

7.
"Hvat er með ásum?
Hvat er með alfum?
Hví ertu einn kominn
í Jötunheima?"

Loki kvað:

"Illt er með ásum,
illt er með alfum;
hefr þú Hlórriða
hamar of folginn?"

Þrymr said:

7.
How are the spirits?
How are the elves?
Why have you come alone
to the home of the ettins?

Loki said:

"The spirits feel bad,
the elves feel bad.
Have you Hlórriða's ("rider of warmth")
rock/hammer hidden?"

Ettin means "big eater" or simply "hunger", from proto-
Nordic *etunaR*, from proto-Germanic *etunaz*.

Þrymr kvað:

8.
"Ek hef Hlórriða.
hamar of folginn
átta röstum
fyr jörð neðan;
hann engi maðr
aftr of heimtir,
nema færi mér
Freyju at kvæn."

8.
"I have Hlórriða's
rock/hammer hidden,
eight rests
under the Earth;
no man
can bring it home,
unless he brings me
Freyja as wife."

A rest is how long you can travel before you need a rest.
Usually about two hours.

9.
Fló þá Loki,
- fjaðrhamr dunði, -
unz fyr útan kom
jötna heima
ok fyr innan kom
ása garða.
Mætti hann Þór
miðra garða,
ok þat hann orða
alls fyrst of kvað:

9.
Loki flew
- the feather-shape thundered -
until he left the home of the ettins,
and entered the yard of the spirits.
He met Þórr
in the middle of the yard,
and he spoke first
of all the words:

10.
"Hefr þú erendi
sem erfiði?
Segðu á lofti
löng tíðendi,
oft sitjanda
sögur of fallask
ok liggjandi
lygi of bellir."

10.

"Have you a troublesome
result?
Tell me in the air
the long news;
often the sitting
forget his tales,
and the lying down
dare lie."

Loki kvað:

11.

"Hef ek erfiði
ok erendi;
Þrymr hefr þinn hamar,
þursa dróttinn;
hann engi maðr
aftr of heimtir,
nema hánum færi
Freyju at kván.

Loki said:

11.
"Have I troublesome
news;
Þrymr has your stone/hammer,
the king of noise,
no man
can bring it home,
unless he brings him
Freyja as wife."

12.
Ganga þeir fagra
Freyju at hitta,
ok hann þat orða
alls fyrst of kvað:
"Bittu þik, Freyja,
brúðar líni;
vit skulum aka tvau
í Jötunheima."

12.
They went to find
the fair Freyja,
and he first of
all said:
"Cover yourself, Freyja,
with the bridal veil,
the two of us are going to
the home of the ettins."

13.
Reið varð þá Freyja
ok fnasaði,
allr ása salr
undir bifðisk,
stökk þat it mikla
men Brísinga:
"Mik veiztu verða
vergjarnasta,
ef ek ek með þér
í Jötunheima."

13.
Freyja was furious
and froze,
the whole hall of spirits
shook,
the shining necklace of fire
fell down.
"Anxious to be married,
they will call me,
if I go with you
to the home of the ettins."

14.
Senn váru æsir
allir á þingi
ok ásynjur
allar á máli,
ok um þat réðu
ríkir tívar
hvé þeir Hlórriða
hamar of sætti.

14.

All the (male and female) spirits,
gathered at the court/Thing,
everyone was there,
and the powerful/rich gods
they discussed,
how they should Hlórriða's
hammer find.

15.

Þá kvað þat Heimdallr,
hvítastr ása,
vissi hann vel fram
sem vanir aðrir:
"Bindum vér Þór þá
brúðar líni,
hafi hann it mikla
men Brísinga.

15.
Heimdallr ("World Tree") then said,
the whitest of spirits,
- he could see far and wide
like the other gods:
"Put the bridal veil
on Þórr,
let him carry
the shining necklace of fire."

16.
Látum und hánum
hrynja lukla
ok kvenváðir
um kné falla,
en á brjósti
breiða steina
ok hagliga
um höfuð typpum."

16.
"Put on him
the key ring,
and women's clothing
to his knees,
put rocks
around his chest
and bind his hair
beautifully on his head."

17.
Þá kvað þat Þór,
þrúðugr áss:
"Mik munu æsir
argan kalla,
ef ek bindask læt
brúðar líni!"

17.
Then Þórr said,
powerful spirit:
"The spirits will
call me a woman
if I put on
the bridal veil!"

18.
Þá kvað þat Loki
Laufeyjar sonr:
"Þegi þú, Þórr,
þeira orða.
Þegar munu jötnar
Ásgarð búa,
nema þú þinn hamar
þér of heimtir."

18.
Then said Loki,
son of foliage:
"Be silent, Þórr,
say no such thing;
soon the ettins come,
to the homes in
the yard of spirits,
if you don't
get your rock/hammer."

19.
Bundu þeir Þór þá
brúðar líni
ok inu mikla
meni Brísinga,
létu und hánum
hrynja lukla
ok kvenváðir
um kné falla,
en á brjósti
breiða steina,
ok hagliga
um höfuð typpðu.

19.
They put the bridal veil
on Þórr
and the shining necklace of fire,
they gave him
the key ring,
and put on him women's clothing
to his knees,
they put rocks on his chest,
and tied his hair beautifully
on his head."

20.
Þá kvað Loki
Laufeyjar sonr:
"Mun ek ok með þér
ambótt vera,
vit skulum aka tvær
í Jötunheima."

20.
Then said Loki,
son of foliage;
"Me as a maid servant,
you will bring,
the two of us as women
will go to the home of the ettins."

21.
Senn váru hafrar
heim of reknir,
skyndir at sköklum,
skyldu vel renna;
björg brotnuðu,
brann jörð loga,
ók Óðins sonr
í Jötunheima.

21.
Quickly the two
goats were brought home,
attached to the poles,
eager to run;
mountains broke,
the Earth burnt,
and Óðinn's son
to the home of the ettins.

22.
Þá kvað þat Þrymr,
þursa dróttinn:
"Standið upp, jötnar,
ok stráið bekki,
nú færa mér
Freyju at kván
Njarðar dóttur
ór Nóatúnum.

22.
Then said Þrymr,
the king of noise:
"Stand up, ettins,
put straw on the benches,
they are now taking to me
Freyja as wife,
daughter of Njörðr
from the court of ships.

23.
Ganga hér at garði
gullhyrnðar kýr,
öxn alsvartir
jötni at gamni;
fjölð á ek meiðma,
fjölð á ek menja,
einnar mér Freyju
ávant þykkir."

23.
Walking here in the yard
cows with golden horns,
pitch black oxen,
ettins against turf-huts;
I have much gold,
I have much treasure,
I now only
want Freyja."

24.
Var þar at kveldi
of komit snemma
ok fyr jötna
öl fram borit;
einn át oxa,
átta laxa,
krásir allar,
þær er konur skyldu,
drakk Sifjar verr
sáld þrjú mjaðar.

24.
They in the evening
came early
and for ettins,
ale was brought forth;
all by himself he (Þórr)
ate one ox,
and eight salmons,
and all the good food
intended for the women,
Sif's husband (Þórr) drank
three kegs of mead.

25.
Þá kvat þat Þrymr,
þursa dróttinn:
"Hvar sáttu brúðir
bíta hvassara?
Sák-a ek brúðir
bíta breiðara,
né inn meira mjöð
mey of drekka."

25.
Then said Þrymr
the king of noise:
"Where did you see bride
bite over more?
Never did I see
bride bite wider
or more mead
any maiden drink."

26.
Sat in alsnotra
ambótt fyrir,
er orð of fann
við jötuns máli:
"Át vætr Freyja
átta nóttum,
svá var hon óðfús
í Jötunheima."

26.
The cunning maiden servant
sat beside him
and found words,
to answer the ettin's speech:
"Freyja didn't eat
for eight nights,
that is how much
she longed for the home of the ettins."

27.
Laut und línu,
lysti at kyssa,
en hann útan stökk
endlangan sal:
"Hví eru öndótt
augu Freyju?
Þykki mér ór augum
eldr of brenna."

27.
He lifted the veil,
wanted a kiss,
but he fell back
to the other side of the hall:
"Why are Freyja's eyes
so sharp?
It looks as if they are on fire."

28.
Sat in alsnotra
ambótt fyrir,
er orð of fann
við jötuns máli:
"Svaf vætr Freyja
átta nóttum,
svá var hon óðfús
í Jötunheima."

28.
The cunning maiden servant
sat beside him
and found words,
to answer the ettin's speech:
"Freyja didn't sleep
for eight nights,
that is how much
she longed for the home of the ettins."

29.
Inn kom in arma
jötna systir,
hin er brúðféar
biðja þorði:
"Láttu þér af höndum
hringa rauða,
ef þú öðlask vill
ástir mínar,
ástir mínar,
alla hylli.

29.
Inn came the old
ettin's sister,
she dared ask for
a bridal present.
"Give me from your hands
red rings,
if you want
love from me,
love from me
and all my hails."

30.
Þá kvað þat Þrymr,
þursa dróttinn:
"Berið inn hamar
brúði at vígja,
lekkið Mjöllni
í meyjar kné,
vígið okkr saman
Várar hendi."

30.
Then said Þrymr,
the king of noise,
"Bring forth the hammer,
to consecrate the bride,
place Mjöllnir (The Crusher)
on the maiden's knee,
and marry us,
with the hands of solemn promises."

31.
Hló Hlórriða
hugr í brjósti,
er harðhugaðr
hamar of þekkði;
Þrym drap hann fyrstan,
þursa dróttin,
ok ætt jötuns
alla lamði.

31.

Laughing in his head,
Hlórriða,
when the tough
felt the hammer in his hand.
He killed Þrymr first,
the king of noise,
and the kin of ettins.

32.

Drap hann ina öldnu
jötna systur,
hin er brúðféar
of beðit hafði;
hon skell of hlaut
fyr skillinga,
en högg hamars
fyr hringa fjölð.
Svá kom Óðins sonr
endr at hamri.

32.
He killed the old
ettin's sister,
who had asked him
for a bridal present.
A slap she got
instead of piles of coins,
and a hammer-strike
instead of wonderful rings.
Thus Óðinn's son
came back to his rock/hammer.

The Interpretation of Þrymskviða

Now that you have seen the shadows dancing on the wall, we will help you turn around and see what is behind.

Þórr's hammer is *his heart*. So when you read that he falls asleep and that while he sleeps someone stole his hammer, he is in fact dead. When he is dead, his heart is lost, and he is cut in two, in a way, a part dwells in his future mother and a part dwells in his future father. Like Persephone.

To return to life, he needs Loki. Loki is what would now be called *hormones*, especially *adrenaline*. He needs Loki to get out of the father, so to speak. But above all, as Loki explains to him, he absolutely needs Freyja, it is only through her that he can find his hammer. Of course, because Freyja is *the egg*.

He needs Freyja through Loki. It is Loki who takes him to Freyja. In other words: the hormones take him to the egg. Or rather to the fact that he realizes that he needs Freyja to live again.

Concerning the giants: it is not that they are very big, it is that you are in a phase of your life where you are very small.

The Jotunheimen giants are ice giants. Ice is the image of something that holds hard in solid form, and then flows. They are rather disgusting. The giants represent what we are calling in our modern words *the endometrium*, the carpet of blood in the womb, so to speak, which is in solid form until menstruations, where it flows, carrying away and cleaning everything in its path.

This endometrium wants above all to have an egg, otherwise it dies. The king of the Jotuns wants to have Freyja.

Loki, the hormones, flies towards this king, in the womb therefore, to ask him to return the hammer. It is true, it was he who stole it, and it is he alone who is able to restore it, since the hammer is life, the heart. But he simply tells the truth when he explains to Loki that he only can return it if he gets Freyja and marries her (if he attaches to her, in other words). Of course, what he doesn't say or doesn't know, is that he needs a *fertilized egg*, so Þórr disguised as Freyja, the picture is perfect. Þórr in the dress of Freyja. The spermatozoa in the egg.

This will also destroy the king, because the endometrium is made to be eaten by the egg or the embryo, and disappear.

Note that the endometrium knew that Loki was coming, he wanted him to come, because only he can bring Freyja. Loki, *a hormone from the ovary here* (*progesterone*: this is why it borrowed the Freyja bird shape after ovulation on the fourteenth day and *the pituitary luteinizing hormone* on the thirteenth day) comes to check if the endometrium is ready to receive the egg, and comes to ensure that it will remain in good condition.

Loki will look for Freyja. Before reaching the uterus seven days later, *the egg is fertilized*, as it is in our modern observations (it is fertilized in *the fallopian tube*).

It is Loki, the progesterone, which makes the uterus able to receive Freyja, and not to destroy the ice giants, because this hormone inhibits the movements of the uterus and allows the endometrium to continue to grow.

It is Freyja who makes the wedding outfit of Þórr. She wraps him and gives him her necklace, the future *umbilical cord*. When Þórr arrives at King Þrymr's home with the progesterone hormone Loki, the king believes he is Freyja. Logic, otherwise he would reject him because the body of the mother, unless it is tricked, should reject any foreign body. In the imaginary, this is why fertilization is done "in secret" in the fallopian tubes. The embryo begins to destroy and "eat" the endometrium by creating enzymes through the future placenta as soon as it arrives on the seventh day (he has no placenta before the seventh day). It is completely installed on the tenth day.

So you understand why Þrymr invites Þórr-Freyja to eat and why he eats eagerly. You understand why Loki, progesterone and *human gonadotropic chorionic hormone* or *pregnancy hormone* (then made by the embryo) attempts to calm Þrymr by tricking him.

King Þrymr gives to Þórr the hammer (life, heart) as soon as he became attached to him. Once he has the hammer, Þórr the embryo destroys the giants, and by their destruction and by fire, he melts them and gets blood from them, and comes out from the womb.

Sources for this book:

-*Samlagets Norrøn ordbok*, 5. utgåva, Oslo 2012

-Snorri Sturluson's *The Eddas*, Þrymskviða

-Hjalmar Falk's, *Etymologisk Ordbog over det norske og det danske Sprog*, Kristiania 1906.

Other books by Varg Vikernes

-*Vargsmål*, Oslo 1997

-*Germansk Mytologi og Verdensanskuelse*, Stockholm 2000

-*Sorcery and Religion in Ancient Scandinavia*, London 2011

-*Reflections on European Mythology and Polytheism*, 2015

-*Mythic Fantasy Role-playing Game (MYFAROG)* v. 2.6, 2015

Other books by Marie Cachet

-*Le secret de l'Ourse*, 2016

-*Le besoin d'impossible*, 2009

Made in the USA
Columbia, SC
16 March 2020